SMITH

SMITH

and other poems by

Tom Rea

1985

DOORYARD PRESS

ACKNOWLEDGEMENTS

Thanks to the editors of the following magazines in which some of these poems, some of them in slightly different versions, first appeared or are forthcoming: *Corona, CutBank, Crazy Horse, The Portland Review*. "Vermeer at an Empty Canvas" first appeared in *Ironwood*. And special thanks to Jane Johnson, David Romtvedt, and Bert Hedin, who helped with the poems.

for Hannah

Smith

Of course, when a man knows well
what he does, it soothes the eye
like balm on a hot sore to watch him:
the long reach of tongs from forge to anvil,
ring of the hammer as it draws
taut curves from the slackened steel
before the plunge
burble and long hiss
of cool.

      He has shaped a loon cry.
The air solidifies around him
when he holds it up, laughing
in the morning work light.
The dying fire leaves
orange spilled across his face.
All the things that hold him there,
cap, skew leather apron, gloves
cuffed to the elbows, glow.

               —for Jug

Leaving the Museum

Sun is leaving a windy parking lot
moving over asphalt
gray with tradition and a dying
time of year:

brown grass by the pavement dying
for a snow blanket, the wind
dying of a killing doubt.
Then the white snow like

manna, the gift
wanted us all along and here
without asking
it comes. Snowflakes arrive

through tumbling branches and dusk
outlining sycamore and balustrade.
Choose your design.
There's nothing new to see

says the museum, turning out its yellow light
craning its big bulk
at the last orange of the day,
secret lover.

Over Vitebsk, *Chagall*

Rumbling by with open doors
a box car empty of everything
moves out of the country, and with it
we head oh, east of early memory
to a green snow time of warming hallways
and confident roads. There
an old man with a cane and a bundle
fills half the winter sky, no longer a slave
to gravity, and relieved
the way a corpse, by the cool
weight of coins, is relieved from seeing
this quiet slush of evening,
church walls and shed roofs
in March. Nearly nothing
can meet the eye while plenty
goes on behind doors and closed shutters:
smell of fresh bread leaking out
to the street, child in a yellow kitchen
far from a gray-green sky
swinging her legs in a yellow high chair
and yelling in pure
relief at the gaping oven door,
smell and heat hurling out in a headlong leaving.

Servant Handing a Letter to her Mistress, *Vermeer*

1.

Fingers to her chin, Klieg–lit from the left
my lady gazes in wonder at the letter
come now, at this of all possible
times. We've abandoned daylight for drama.

Such pearls! Such ermine!
The yellow silk of her gown
rustles and gleams. Here you are,
my lady. My lady's gaze

naive for her finery, not quite coy
falls on the central prop, the letter
while the plot
whirls and circles around her.

2.

In fact, the scoundrel is gentleman enough to inform
her that, though he will love her to his deathbed, he
must return to his wife and business in Brussels,
and he trusts that with her beauty and breeding she
will have no trouble finding a suitable father for his
child.

3.

Here you are my lady.
My lady has not yet read the news, remember,
and the news in its gleaming
white packet weighs in the servant's hand,
hot lead.

Here, you are my lady
always, and I your servant,
and if my cheeks are ruddy
it's from sun and honest scrub-work, and if
the dun of my gown fades
unremarkably into the black background
no matter. For I have read the letter
and the taste of what I know and you do not
will linger, this moment
will change your life and you
will remember always, clearer
than the man, the night, or the glowing
clarity of your own young skin,
me, the one who brought the news.

Cape Cod Afternoon, *Hopper*

Blocks of light on the big house slant
crazy off pitched roofs and gable ends.
The green lawn breathes a lungful of ocean.

Someone has left a window open
a black square calling, Supper!
and down at the beach in seaweed,

in rocks and tide pools, a child
takes a lazy poke at a starfish.
He's lost a sneaker and the scheme

to blame it on his brother. He drags
a stick in the sand for a snake track,
wiggly first, then wide curves. Gulls rise,

scream off toward Spain.
Down at the harbor his friend Louie
the Portugese crabber tells him

"Lose a shoe it floats to Africa,
maybe you get a letter back." Water is flat
around the boats, with rainbows. You can smell

sun on the dock wood. Here by the splintery part
those summer people crashed their boat
all laughing right up against. A lady

fell in and the sail went shivering crazy.
The sky that day was orange, his brother
found a clearie in the road that matched it.

Round and clear, like Daddy's Navy song
O the ocean waves may roll...
The lawn is turning gold now,

his bare foot chilly. Looking up
the house, the thinning light, he waves
at the empty air.

Waves and waves like flags
in the Bristol parade when music
quits. Feet and the thumping drums.

Vermeer at an Empty Canvas

In another quarter hour, red
will come up on the rug and the sun
hit the wineglass. Memory
is egg and oil and color:
the girl's eye
flicks her lover's in the mirror;
light bulks alive in the milkmaid's forearm,
begins in the stream from jug to bowl.
Yesterday, a long
walk along the water watching boats
tack up the sound. When I came in
Maria turned from the corner by the window
her hand on the sill like that.
Behind her the corner began to move
the wall bowed in big waves
I reeled, the floor
held its pattern and I grabbed
a chair for balance.
                         This
is the best part, this white square,
air through the window. I breathe
and hold it, house and day
pivot slowly around me.
The quiet grows, builds
solid figures out of air,
voices for the room,
voices for the room behind that.

Little Whispers

Little whispers come at night
when I'm falling asleep, little
whispers I nearly remember next day,
recalling shapes and cadences but never
the words, never the whole
program a friend of mine once said
who in his walleyed way could watch
all sides of the sky at once, so that
nothing airborne ever escaped him—
swallow, butterfly, jet (he could read
signs in the contrails)—though what
he knew of rocks and earthworms, grass
and sandy anthills was badly
limited I would remind myself.
When he talked, when he told
of all he saw I remember
looking up at the phone wires
stretched around that treeless neighborhood
by the sea,
the parallel sags between poles,
and a few black longtailed birds, quarter notes
in an unsyncopated song for the little sister
I never had but who followed me everywhere
with a cup of dirt.
                    She was our bait carrier,
night crawlers, and she would whisper,
knowing it better than either of us
how if you hurt one, cut off its tail maybe,
it could always grow another.

A Girl Asleep, *Vermeer*

1.

Beyond the chair, the table
with its rich carpet, homely pitcher and fruit
beyond the lovely girl leaning asleep on her hand

beyond the half-open door
the highlighted door jamb
lies another room, nearly empty

with a warm brown floor.

2.

At a summer camp where
to take a boat out on your own you have to first
swim the lake

a boy goes down to the shore each morning early,
before the bell or any breeze
and dreams himself
gliding alone in a green canoe
to the call of a swamp frog, peep of a rat
quiet paddle-ripple
quiet wake.

3.

She is dreaming him ages off
swimming easily
and though she will forget him when she wakes
the green, deep lake will stay with her
and with her the feel
of his young muscles, strong and relaxed
moving him through it, of the water
swirling and bubbling quietly all around him.

By the Stock Pond

Late, late at night when I was young
I would put my ear to my pillow and listen
every night for thunder, and only
years later would I know it for
my own pulse.

        And now that I hear it
less often I'm less sure of the fact.
For what I've come to know
like thunder is that facts
are what we wander away with

just when the world gets interesting:
there is a drum in the ear; a killdeer's
peep to his mate we call the ballad-word
plaintive, as though sorrow
had any place at an evening mud-pond on the prairie.

Plum

Snow can fall
softly, as if down
were its direction only
by accident, the way
when you entered a room
my great aunt Marian
would look up, old eyes
bulgy and dim behind
thick lenses, the accident
of the two of you in the same room
unremarkable, if soothing.

Maybe she'd lick
a stamp or straighten
the antimacassar, not
thinking how her daughter
died alone in a room
with the shades pulled down.
One day when I'm
home on a Christmas visit
my father will give me
that same look
and say "Oh"
only slightly surprised,
the one round vowel
hung between us like a plum
that knows its own
ripeness, and exactly
when to fall.

That Same Father

whose hair I'd smell
the creases of whose forehead I'd lay my fingers in
as he bore me tall and slipping on his shoulders
into the waves on rolling August afternoons when I was four
to the salt weight of the sea

listens closely to his heart, neck bent
and shuffles the blue carpet
crossing through the window daylight. He touches
the glass with the pitcher he pours from, or he'll miss:
one eye is bad.

That same father
who in the dark of our roomette when I was six on the sleeper bound
west to Pittsburgh, woke me with his bony elbow
so I could see, moonlit silver, straight across the Horseshoe's U
the diesel, heading back from where we headed
but pulling us.

Her Traveling Son Writes Home

My dearest Mother
you know when they show movies of clouds
passing with their shadows
all speeded up over the Grand Canyon,
how the mottled purples, browns and grays
churn like years passing?
Like children
never turning out quite
how you'd expected, or even desired?

On such a morning I dreamed
your mottled skin.
Your tired legs, weary and veined
rested nude on a pink ottoman,
there was a plate with some half-eaten crackers
and the silverware drawer was only half-closed,
a few glints muffled in brown flannel.

I do not understand
the expectant feeling. All your gracious walls
were suddenly covered by the wrong paintings:
Mont-St.-Michel in a shimmery, sentimental dusk,
as if the bright stink of the tide flats
were smothered by cut chrysanthemums
in a small room.

The Black and the Dazzle

Some winter mornings
dawn a wild, dazzling bright
finding and blessing everything—
fence post, phone pole
brown grasses poking through snow,
brown cattail medley at the frozen marsh—
with its particular self.
The cold air holds nothing
but transparent possibility.
My daughter
beside me on the seat
chatters along of what she remembers
of summer, the races we had
in the yard on her birthday.
We pass a snowplow, coming at us
and find ourselves for a panicked second
with nothing but each other.
My father writes:
"I am deteriorating steadily and painlessly."
Again the road appears, with
mailboxes, pollarded trees around a farmhouse
and a black line of cattle
strung feeding along a line of hay.

500 copies of *Smith* were printed during a cold November by Barbara Rea. The paper is Arches. The Garamond type was set by the author wearing a hat.